The ABC's of Adulting

First paperback edition December 2020

Book design by Samantha Kellian Smith

978-1-953323-08-8 (paperback)
978-1-953323-04-0 (hardcover)
978-1-953323-07-1 (ebook)

This book is dedicated to the many people who were forced to read and edit it over a four year time period: Noel, Jaclyn, Kayla, Emily, Steve, Erica, Isaac, and Stephanie to name a few. Also to Kegan for agreeing to play the part of illustrator after much begging and pleading.

larm Clock

The thing you will grow to hate. A lot. As it will be waking you up about 6 hours earlier than you are used to.

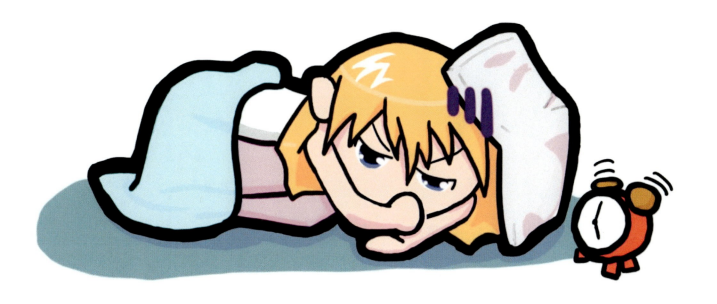

Little Peggy just started a job in corporate finance. Now, her alarm clock rings at 5AM to wake her up... just in time to sit in traffic for 2 hours!

Behave

Now that you're an adult, there are certain adult standards to which you will be held at social events.

Little Peggy used to have so much fun drinking at parties, stealing shot glasses, and sneaking into Taco Bell at 2am. Now that she's an adult, illegal Taco Bell exploits are highly discouraged.

Cooking

No more college dining halls for you! If you want to eat nutritiously, you'll need to learn how to make more than macaroni and cheese.

Little Peggy is feeling very malnourished because she had only eaten boxed pasta for two months... so she is teaching herself how to cook salmon and asparagus.

ebt

Something you will have a lot of.

Little Peggy was sad because her student loans put her bank account into the negative. Now she is even more sad because she also needs to pay for rent, car insurance, and buy an adorable pumpkin Halloween costume for her cat.

Energy

Something you will start having less and less of.

DROOL

Little Peggy used to be able to stay out until 3 am every night drinking and having fun! Now she goes to bed at 9.

F at

You will now be sitting at a desk all day. You will probably get fat. Like... more than the freshman 15.

Little Peggy used to run every day, go to Zumba, and play pick up volleyball with her friends. Now her only exercise is doing leg lifts under her desk. She has already gained 45 pounds.

Garbage

That stuff you need to take out to the curb once a week, along with doing your other new adult-typed chores.

Little Peggy has so many new chores now that she is an adult! Her first lesson learned was to invest in heavy-duty garbage bags. The cheap ones did not work out so well...

Homework

What you don't need to do any more! Don't get too excited though... your job will take more time than your homework did.

Little Peggy was so exited to not have to write any more English papers! That is, until she realized she would have to work 14 hours just to put together one client Power Point presentation.

Interviews

What you'll be doing a lot of if you want to land a job and make money. Get ready to be forced into socialization!

Little Peggy does not like people, nor does she want to socialize with them. However, she had to suck it up and pretend to be a good conversationalist in order to trick her interviewers into giving her a job.

J ob

If you do all those interviews, just maybe, you'll get a job. This is what you'll do to make money to afford your new adult lifestyle.

Little Peggy landed herself a high paying job after doing so well in her interviews. Now she gets to sit in a cubical all day surrounded by paperwork!

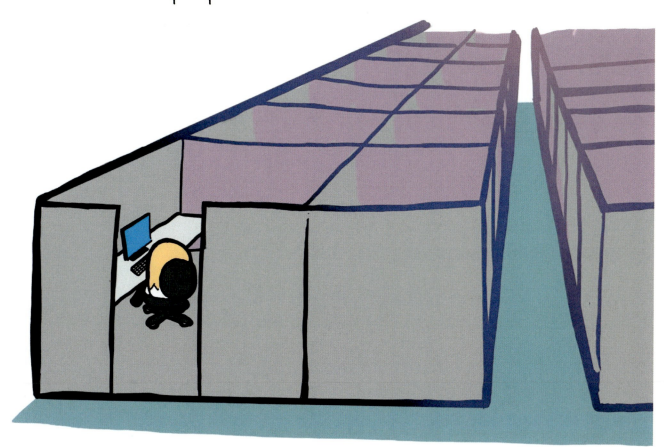

Kiss-ass

What you'll need to do to get ahead in that new job of yours.

Little Peggy really wanted a promotion because she needed more money to pay for her IKEA furniture and cat, so she started complimenting her boss every morning and bringing in coffee every afternoon.

Laundry

Learn how to work that detergent, fabric softener, and bleach! Don't expect there to be a washer and dryer in your apartment.

Little Peggy was teaching herself how to do laundry. Unfortunately she didn't realize it would involve a 3 hour wait at the laundromat or turning all of her clothes pink!

Move

What you'll have to do, most likely on your own, when you want to switch apartments. Be sure to make friends with someone who owns a truck.

Little Peggy decided to move into a new apartment. Unfortunately, this required multiple weekends of taking apart and re-building all of her Ikea furniture.

News

Now that you're an adult, you can't live in a bubble! You have to be a functioning member of society who knows about things like the Dow and China.

Little Peggy spends every morning watching the news while she eats breakfast. That way, she can pretend to have an informed discussion with her boss about the world when she gets to work.

On top of things

How you need to seem to the outside world.
All. Of. The. Time.

Although she is dying on the inside, little Peggy always projects an air of confidence and control, tricking those around her into thinking that she knows what she is doing.

Parents

The people who will no longer be paying for your activities, food, or rent. But don't worry. They still love you. Maybe…

Little Peggy's parents decided to charge her $300 rent to live at home for 2 weeks. She is not amused.

Quit

What you can't do now that you're an adult and need money.

Little Peggy hates her job. She wants to quit. She can't quit because her job pays her money. She likes the money.

Roommate

Roommates are essential if you would like to afford your new hole-in-the-wall apartment.

Little Peggy had to find a roommate so she could afford her apartment. Her roommate is nice... except when he comes home at 3am on a Wednesday night, turns on all the lights, and decides to make a quesadilla.

Soul

What will be slowly sucked out of you at your new job.

Little Peggy just spent 10 hours checking data in a massive Excel spreadsheet on her fancy computer at work. She is now a zombie.

Taxes

Things you get to file yourself because you have a job! You will be confused.

Little Peggy tried to do her taxes. She has no idea if she did them correctly and is hoping that she won't get audited (whatever that means).

Umbrella

Now that you're an adult you should probably buy one of these.

Little Peggy has to get to work,
but it is raining. Because she forgot
to do her adulting, she doesn't have
an umbrella and has to go to work
looking like a wet cat.

Vent

You are going to want to vent a lot. About everything. How tired you are. How poor you are. How difficult your life is. Do not do this around your judgmental friends.

Little Peggy is tired, so tired, and very poor, and stressed out. She tried telling her friend, but instead her friend went on a 45 minute rant about how much more tired she was than Little Peggy.

Wait

Much of adulting is spent wasting your time waiting for various things. It is the opposite of fun.

Little Peggy waited 4 hours at the DMV to register her car. Then she spent 50 minutes on hold with Comcast. Now she has to wait in line at Starbucks because she forgot to order her Mocha Latte on the app.

Xerox

That strange machine in the corner of the office that you will most likely need to know how to work. It is used to make copies of things.

Little Peggy tried to use the Xerox machine to make copies of her boss' confidential documents. Instead, she has printed 1,000 copies to every floor of her building. Needless to say, her boss' documents are no longer confidential.

Yes

How you will respond to any request from your boss. All the time.

Little Peggy's boss asked her to work for 10 hours over the weekend and shred 72 boxes of paper. Little Peggy said 'Yes'.

Zero

The number of fuc….arts that you're NOT allowed to give at your new job.

Little Peggy gave zero farts about her new job and slept at her desk all day. Subsequently, she was fired, lost her source of income, and had to move back in with her parents. But that's ok, she was fine not being an adult for just a little longer.

Samantha Smith is an ex-financial analyst/voice-over-artist/program-manager/MBA/author. She wrote this book out of boredom on a plane after spending 5 years adulting in the corporate finance world. She lives in Seattle and spends most days trying to remind herself to not take adulting too seriously.

Kegan Smith is a Boston artist who likes to dabble in all things creative. He loves to stream and play videogames and get pestered by his sister to draw stuff for her books. You can catch him on Twitch under the screen name \bssix.